MAGIC WRAPPA

THE LIGHT WITHIN YOU

AS I THINK, SO I AM
Proverbs 23:7

THIS BOOK BELONGS TO

____

OF THE ROYAL FAMILY

Daily declarations to glow your light:

I AM STRONG

I AM SMART

I AM BEAUTIFUL

I AM WONDERFULLY MADE

I AM

I AM IN HEAVEN EVERY DAY

MAGIC: having super powers

WRAPPA: a wrap to cover your body

MAGIC WRAPPA: a Supernatural covering

Magic Wrappa was made using the image and likeness of my beautiful family.

Dear MargeryGrace - Obutor, the super star... never stop beaming.

Category: Juvenile Fiction.
This is a work of creative nonfiction, however, some parts have been fictionalized in varying degrees, for various purposes.

Names: Eligwe, Marcia, author | Umeike, Ugonna, illustrator.
Title: Magic Wrappa: The Light Within You
Summary: *"Magic Wrappa is a faith-based Children's Book Series that introduces young readers to their rich cultural heritage in Christ, through the adventures of a Super Cloth."* - Publisher

For Educators:
When five year old Obutor loses Wrappa - the physical and spiritual gift she was given at birth - a search causes her to evolve as she finds so much more in its history and in its purpose. Obu is inspired to share all the things she learns about herself and her heritage by leaving magical stories like this one, for future generations.

Published by Heaven Projects Publishing:
Heaven Projects is a division of Em&M Solutions LLC

ISBN 978-1-960228-01-7 (paperback) | ISBN 978-1-960228-03-1 (hardcover)

www.MarciaPrince.com

Heaven Projects Presents

Magic Wrappa

The Light Within You

Created by Marcia Eligwe

Illustrated by Ugonna Umeike

Heaven Projects Publishing

ONCE UPON A TIME...

In a small village you have never heard of,
lived a grand Mama full of magic and love.

She flew over seas
with her gifts to adorn
A brand new baby
on the day I was born.

TAKE CARE OF HER.
YES, MAMA.
IT IS THE TRADITION TO INHERIT A MOTHER'S WRAPPA; THE SAME SWADDLE GRANDMAMA HAD USED TO WRAP HER.

I grew up with Wrappa;

it never hit the ground.

Obutor
IT'S A WHOLE NEW WORLD!
Every day was Heaven
when Wrappa was around.

THEN, ONE DAY...

I went to Mama's village on a plane but on the way, I lost Wrappa so the rich green skies turned gray. Mama promised me a better one, yet I was still blue. My Wrappa was magical, and no one had a clue!

IS THAT A BIRD...?
NO, A FLYING WRAPPA.
SEE YA LATER!

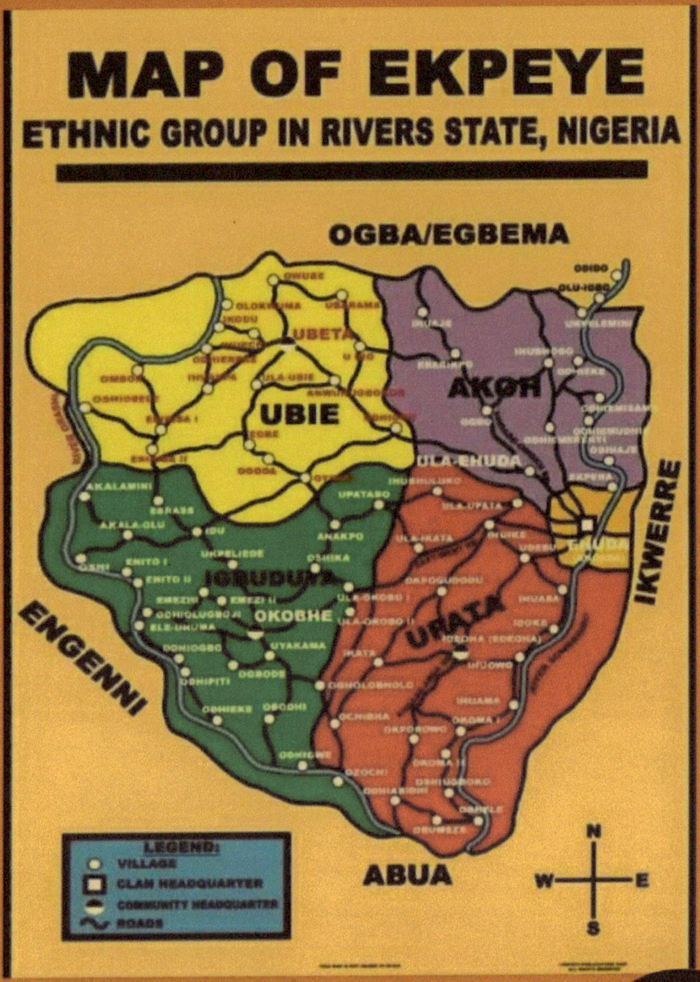

My tears gave me
strength when I
wished Wrappa
was still here;

Mama tripled
that power with
her words in my ear:

OBUTOR!
"Your name in a native tongue you never knew, Means 'Happiness', which is always within you!"
JUST LOOK INSIDE!

SO I OPENED UP MY HEART,
AND I COULD FINALLY SEE...
A magic Wrappa wardrobe
was Mama's best secret!
One wrap and a tuck made
them all a perfect fit.
OBU IS HERE!

Wrappas could be any
thing, and to my surprise
Each one transformed
right before my eyes.

With that Wrappa on
your head rolled like a bun,
You could carry the world
in a pot just for fun.

She taught me
to balance loads
with no slip;

Mama did
all of this,

With a baby
on her hip!

When you twirl Wrappa around layers from left to right,

You can tie a **WRAPPA POCKET**

...and tuck money inside.

WRAP IT! as a skirt;

WRAP IT! on your crown;

OCHOCHO!
WHAT A HAPPY SPIRIT!
Wrappa will make you the JOY of the whole town.

When I was tired, Mama
carried me on her back
And tied Wrappa around
me like a baby in a sack.
I was afraid 'til her
fingers creeped
up to play;

Her tight knots and tickles

drove all fears away.

'TIL MIDNIGHT,

I got to play
Àdaezè
at pretend
Village Ball;

Complete with a crown
that could not fall.
One sparkly Wrappa
was all Mama needed

To make me
a ball gown
just in time
for bed.

At the end of my visit, as I packed up to leave,
Mama gave me a new coat; I could not believe

This special gift was such a wonder to behold.
I wished to be Wrappa; it was unlike any mold.
I AM A STAR.

...Mama had sewed Wrappa pieces on my clothes for the road. Each one made me feel so brand-new.

ÙGBÈDÈ!
YES, SHE IS.
OH!
MAMA'S CRAFT WAS TOO GRAND TO BE TRUE.

I FINALLY KNEW THE TRUTH,

Wrappa is a treat with a simple trick;
Power fills you the moment you **Believe**:
Every fabric carries Mama Magic!

...SO SHE GREW OLD WEARING WRAPPAS
& JUST LIKE MAMA SHOWED, HAPPILY SPREADS
OBUTOR MAGIC! WITH A PENCIL & HER THREADS.
PRINCE
COOLEST MOM EVER!
MOMMY'
OLD
WRAPPAS
THE END
by Obutor

GLOSSARY

OBU'S MAGIC WORDS

- ★ ADAEZE: Princess; the daughter of a King. [Ekpeye].
- ★ ADORN: to make more beautiful; crown with glory.
- ★ ELIGWE: Heaven. [Ekpeye].
- ★ HEAVEN: a state of utmost happiness.
- ★ NATIVE: belonging to a person by birth.
- ★ OBUTOR: Happiness. [Ekpeye].
- ★ SPIRIT: the nonphysical part of a being; a supernatural frame of mind.
- ★ TONGUE: a person's way of speaking.
- ★ TRADITION: beliefs that are passed down to generations.
- ★ TRANSFORMED: change in character or condition.
- ★ UBETA: a village in the region of Rivers, Nigeria.
- ★ UGBEDE NUZO: "Beauty Arise"; used to encourage or speak life and beauty into any person or thing. [Ekpeye].
  /oog.beh.deh-nu.zoh/
- ★ VILLAGE: a small place where people live, or a community of people.
- ★ WARDROBE: a large cabinet or room where clothes may be hung or stored.
- ★ WRAPPA: a cloth fabric used to wrap; a covering for your body. [English: Wrapper]

[Language of Origin]

Anyone Can Wear Wrappa!

What you need: 1 magic fabric

[Just follow these simple steps]

1.

Grab a handful of each Wrappa corner and hold it up behind your backside.

2.

Pull the Wrappa to the side you want your knot. Line it up against your waist or hips.

3.

Cross both ends over each other.

4.

Pull one end through the opening and tighten.

5.

Tie more knots if you want to, but that's it.

Girl or Boy,
Shine with Joy
just like Wrappa!

ILLUSTRATED BY
VCMOR ELIGWE

CREATOR'S NOTE

Marcia was born in Georgia to Nigerian Parents and currently makes her home in Texas. As an Ekpeye girl, Nigerian American and Believer, she writes about cultures and their deep connection to one's faith and identity.

Magic Wrappa is infused with references from Marcia's favorite fairy tales, Bible stories and childhood memories.; how many can you identify?
A great hope is that wherever any fabric reaches, Wrappa's story also follows and releases the magic within YOU.

This book will connect people all over the world and bring them back home to discover who they are in their self and in their spirit. Only then, can we all begin to walk in our purpose and **Shine Bright Like Wrappa!**

This Magic Wrappa is dedicated to:
Sister Esther, Aunty Patience, and Grandpapa.
Thank you for the inspiration to write a truth that transcends life.

ESTHER ETUK. PATIENCE EDOHOUKWA. CHIEF MORGAN OGIRI.

"I LOVE YOU ALL."

May you realize how much the future depends on your Story.

MARCIA PRINCE ELIGWE

I AM magic
YES YOU ARE!

MAGIC WRAPPA
THE LIGHT WITHIN YOU

MY STORY IS MY SUPERPOWER

(Create and Color Your Own Story with Obu)

My name is ______________________

I am from the land of ______________________

My name is special and it means ______________________
(hint: you can make up a new name or your own meaning)

____

____

____

(Draw a picture to show you being YOU!)

My Wrappa© is unique like me, and it looks like this:

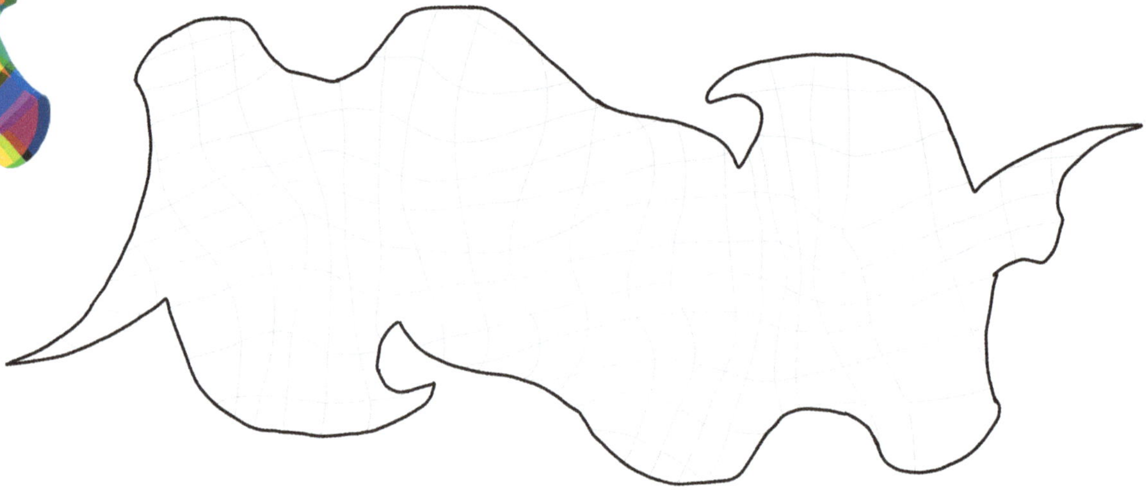

This Magic Wrappa© is Spirit because it lives inside of me

with my __________ talents, and my __________ thoughts.

I can have __________ like Wrappa and be anything I dream.

I just have to Imagine It and Believe It.

(Consider passing down this book and your Magic Wrappa to a friend or stranger.)

What a great way for you to live on through your story. Oh, the places you'll go!

www.MagicWrappa.com

DO NOT TEAR. SHARE INSTEAD.

Ingram Content Group UK Ltd.
Milton Keynes UK
UKHW051102310323
419447UK00004B/90

* 9 7 8 1 9 6 0 2 2 8 0 3 1 *